Manatees

Manatees

A Carolrhoda Nature Watch Book

by Sally M. Walker

Carolrhoda Books, Inc. / Minneapolis

For Erin Wayman and Howie, her adopted manatee, and for Therese Nickels, another manatee fan

The author and publisher gratefully acknowledge the generous assistance of Cathy Beck, wildlife biologist at the U.S. Geological Survey, Sirenia Project.

Carolrhoda Books, Inc.
A Division of the Lerner Publishing Group
241 First Avenue North, Minneapolis, MN 55401 U.S.A.

Website address: www.lernerbooks.com

LIBRARY OF CONGRESS CATALOGING-IN-PUBLICATION DATA

Walker, Sally M.
    Manatees / by Sally M. Walker.
        p.   cm.
    "A Carolrhoda nature watch book."
    Includes index.
    Summary: Describes the physical characteristics, life cycle, behavior, and conservation of manatees, also known as sea cows.
    ISBN 1–57505–299–7 (alk. paper)
    1. Manatees—Juvenile literature. [1. Manatees.
2. Endangered species.] I. Title.
QL737.S63W25 1999
599.55—dc21   98-31325

Manufactured in the United States of America
1 2 3 4 5 6 – JR – 04 03 02 01 00 99

CONTENTS

A GENTLE SEA ANIMAL

For more than two thousand years, sailors have told tales about mermaids, beautiful, long-haired creatures who were half woman, half fish. In 1493, while sailing in the Caribbean Sea near the island later called Hispaniola, Christopher Columbus wrote that his crew had seen three mermaids rising up out of the water. Many fantastic creatures live in the ocean. Did Columbus's crew really see mermaids?

The sailors may have seen manatees, large, gentle **mammals** that live in water. Manatees really don't look much like people—they look more like walruses. Dim light or fog may have fooled Columbus's men into thinking they had spotted mermaids, and their experience probably made a great story to tell the folks back at home. But the truth about manatees is also a great story, one that is strange, interesting, and sometimes sad.

This dugong looks similar to a manatee, but one main difference is the dugong's notched tail. Compare it to the manatee's round tail on page 6.

Many people call manatees "sea cows" because they eat grasses. Biologists, or scientists who study living things, have another way of describing manatees. To biologists, manatees are known as sirenians—members of an order, or scientific grouping, called Sirenia. The name *Sirenia* comes from Greek mythology. Sirens were women whose songs enchanted sailors, luring their ships onto rocks. Millions of years ago, there were dozens of **species,** or kinds, of sirenians. Only four are left: three species of manatees and one species of their relatives, the dugongs (DOO-gongs).

At a quick glance, manatees and dugongs look very much alike, but they're easy to tell apart once you know what to look for. A dugong's tail flipper is notched in the middle, while a manatee's is not. Another difference is that dugongs have tusks, or sharp teeth, in their upper jaw. (Only the male dugong's tusks are long enough to stick out beyond his upper lip.)

Although sirenians live in the water and look somewhat like walruses, they aren't related to walruses or to any other living **aquatic,** or water-dwelling, mammals. In fact, sirenians' closest living relatives are elephants, aardvarks, and hyraxes—all land dwellers! All these animals share a land-dwelling ancestor that lived about 55 to 60 million years ago.

Sirenians look like they might be related to the walrus (below), *but their closest relatives are actually the hyrax* (above), *the elephant* (top right), *and the aardvark* (bottom right).

Gradually, some of this ancestor's descendants began to spend time in the water, perhaps in search of food. Their watery new **habitat,** or the place where an animal normally lives and grows, led to several changes in body shape. During the next 5 to 10 million years, their front legs slowly changed into flippers, their hind legs disappeared, and their tail developed into a powerful paddle.

9

Florida (top left) *and Antillean* (bottom left) *manatees are commonly photographed in their natural habitats. The Amazonians below are in captivity. West African manatees are rarely photographed.*

The first animal that resembled modern manatees lived about 15 million years ago. Although there were many species of manatees in ancient times, only three remain: West Indian *(Trichechus manatus)*, West African *(Trichechus senegalensis)*, and Amazonian *(Trichechus inunguis)*.

West Indian manatees are divided into two subspecies. The Florida manatee *(Trichechus manatus latirostris)* lives along the coast of the southeastern United States. Florida manatees range as far north as Virginia and as far west as Louisiana. The Antillean manatee *(Trichechus manatus manatus)* lives in calm, shallow coastal waters in the Caribbean, along the northeastern coast of South America, and sometimes as far north as southern Texas.

As their name suggests, West African manatees live along the coasts and in the rivers of West Africa, from Senegal to Angola. Amazonian manatees, the third species, live only in freshwater. They live in South America's Amazon River and in the rivers, lakes, and canals that feed into it.

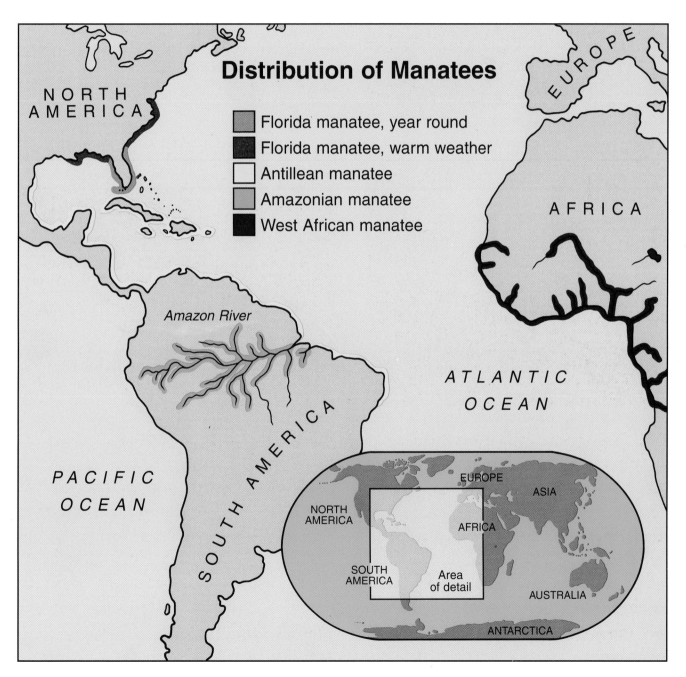

Distribution of Manatees

- Florida manatee, year round
- Florida manatee, warm weather
- Antillean manatee
- Amazonian manatee
- West African manatee

NORTH AMERICA

EUROPE

AFRICA

Amazon River

ATLANTIC OCEAN

PACIFIC OCEAN

SOUTH AMERICA

EUROPE

ASIA

NORTH AMERICA

AFRICA

SOUTH AMERICA

Area of detail

AUSTRALIA

ANTARCTICA

A modern drawing of a Steller's sea cow, a sirenian that is extinct because of overhunting by humans

Until the 1760s, there was a fifth species of sirenian, the Steller's sea cow. This large animal reached lengths of as much as 26 feet (7.9 m), more than twice the length of living sirenians. Russian sailors discovered the Steller's sea cow in 1741, when they were shipwrecked in the Aleutian Islands off the coast of Alaska. Heavily hunted, Steller's sea cows were **extinct,** or all gone, by 1768.

The number of manatees left in the world is unknown. A Florida manatee count in early 1998 found that at least 2,022 individuals remain. No total counts have been made of Amazonian or West African manatees. Biologists estimate that their numbers range from several hundred to several thousand. All three manatee species are **endangered,** or threatened with extinction, and it is against the law to hurt or kill them.

Right: *Manatees are endangered, even though laws have been passed to protect them.*

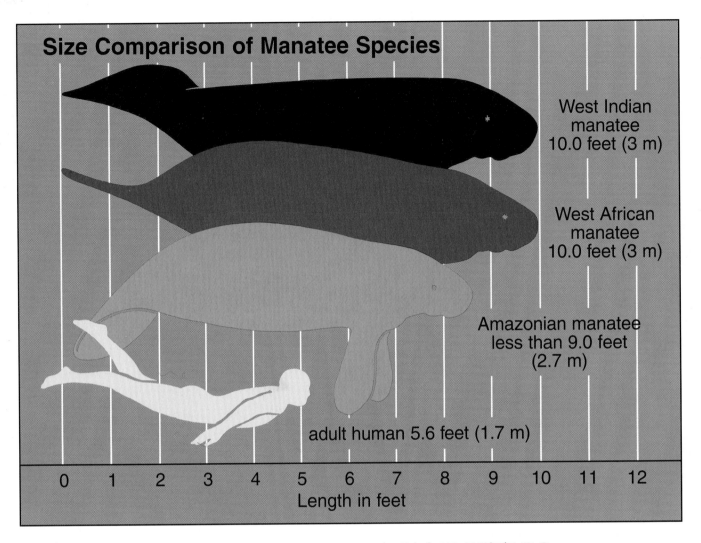

Size Comparison of Manatee Species

West Indian manatee 10.0 feet (3 m)

West African manatee 10.0 feet (3 m)

Amazonian manatee less than 9.0 feet (2.7 m)

adult human 5.6 feet (1.7 m)

0 1 2 3 4 5 6 7 8 9 10 11 12
Length in feet

PHYSICAL CHARACTERISTICS

Florida manatees and Antillean manatees, the two West Indian subspecies, can't be told apart just by looking at them from the outside. Biologists have divided them into subspecies based on differing measurements of certain areas of their skulls. In other ways, however, the two subspecies are very much alike.

Both average 10 feet (3.0 m) in length and about 1,200 pounds (545 kg) in weight. Florida manatees may be as long as 13 feet (4.0 m) and weigh as much as 3,500 pounds (1,590 kg), while Antillean manatees may reach 11.5 feet (3.5 m) and weigh up to 2,200 pounds (1,000 kg).

The snout of the West Indian manatee (above) slants downward more than that of the Amazonian (left) or West African manatee.

West African manatees are about the same size and weight as West Indian manatees. They also look very similar, except that a West African manatee's eyes bulge a bit more than those of a West Indian manatee, and West Africans have blunter snouts. The bones of the West African manatee's snout slant downward less than those of the West Indian manatee, too.

Amazonian manatees are smaller than the other two species. They average less than 9 feet in length (2.7 m). The largest recorded Amazonian manatee was only 9.2 feet (2.8 m). Amazonian manatees are also slimmer than other manatees. One large individual weighed 1,056 pounds (480 kg). Another difference is that the Amazonian manatee's snout bones slant downward even less than those of the West African manatee.

Whatever their size, manatees are built for life underwater. They have broad chests, and their bodies gradually get slimmer toward the tail. This shape allows water to flow easily around a manatee's body as it swims. Manatees can twist, somersault, swim upside down, and move vertically (up and down) in the water.

Manatees have flat, paddle-shaped tails. As a manatee moves its tail up and down, powerful muscles push the animal through the water. Manatees usually swim at speeds ranging from 2 to 6 miles per hour (3.2–9.7 km/hr). When frightened, they may put on bursts of speed above 15 miles per hour (24.1 km/hr).

Manatee bones are dense and heavy, so they help the animal sink underwater. Another feature that helps a manatee rise and sink is its long lungs, which are located along its back, beneath the spine.

When the lungs are filled with air, they help the manatee remain horizontal in the water. They work much the way that a styrofoam float strapped to a child's back keeps the child afloat. When a manatee wants to go deeper, it contracts, or squeezes, its lung muscles. Squeezed air takes up less space, so the manatee sinks. When the manatee relaxes the lung muscles, the lungs and the air inside them expand. Like a balloon released underwater, the manatee rises.

Manatees are graceful swimmers.

A manatee can simply poke its nostrils out of the water when it needs to take a breath (left). *The nostrils are covered with flaps of skin when the manatee is underwater* (above).

Manatees do not need to breathe as frequently as people do, which is important since they spend a lot of time underwater. On average, manatees breathe about every 2 to 4 minutes. While resting or sleeping, they breathe less frequently. A resting adult may stay underwater for as much as 20 minutes. Its nostrils, which are about the size of a dime, are covered by flaps of skin that close like valves while the manatee is underwater. When it resurfaces, the manatee needs only to stick its nostrils into the air to suck in a breath. The rest of the manatee's body stays submerged.

A manatee's flippers come in handy at mealtime. Notice the nails on the end of this Florida manatee's flippers.

The hind legs that the manatee's ancient ancestor used for walking have disappeared, and the ancestor's front legs have become flippers. West African and West Indian manatees have three or four flattened nails, sort of like a human's fingernails, on each flipper. Amazonian manatees have no nails. Their flippers are also longer than those of the other species.

A manatee uses its flippers in several ways. It can use them to walk along the bottom of a waterway or to pull or push itself up to reach food. By bending its flippers, a manatee can clutch plants, then lift and shove them into its mouth.

Because a manatee has flippers to help it reach and grab plants, it doesn't need to turn or bend its head much to eat. That's a good thing, because manatees have only six **cervical vertebrae,** spinal column bones found in the neck area. Most other mammals, including the long-necked giraffe, have seven. Mammals with fewer vertebrae have trouble turning their heads. A manatee's six vertebrae are so closely spaced that it can turn its head only a small amount. If a manatee wants to look behind itself, it usually must turn its body.

Manatees can appear to be walking, even though they have no legs. This manatee is using its flippers to pull itself along the bottom of a waterway.

Manatees have rough skin that may be up to 2 inches (5.1 cm) thick. While West Indian and West African manatees have wrinkly skin, Amazonians are smoother. All three species have hairs scattered over their bodies and short, stiff bristles on their snouts.

The rough, thick skin of a manatee might remind you of the manatee's relative, the elephant.

Manatees range from gray to brown in color. Amazonian manatees have white or pink patches on their stomach and chest. Sometimes manatees look greenish because of the algae that grow on their bodies. Algae are small, green organisms, or life forms, that live in the water. Barnacles, a type of saltwater shellfish, also latch onto manatee skin. Manatees rid themselves of algae and barnacles by sloughing off, or shedding, sheets of dead skin. Sometimes the skin falls off on its own or is rubbed off by flowing water. Skin is also sloughed off when manatees scratch themselves against the sandy bottoms of their waterways.

This manatee isn't really green—it just has algae growing on its body.

Biologists believe that manatees see fairly well. Their eyes have tiny, light-sensitive cells called **rods** and **cones.** Rods help animals see well in dim light, while cones help them tell colors apart. Manatees can see objects clearly, even underwater. Since manatees have cones, biologists think they may be able to see colors, too.

Manatees have two ways of protecting their eyes. Like people, manatees have eyelids, but their eyelids don't blink up and down like people's do. Instead, the muscles around the eyes contract and release in a circular motion. When a manatee dives, a special membrane, or tissue, called a **nictitating membrane** slides up over each eye. The membranes protect the eyes from being poked by plants and grasses, but they don't lessen vision.

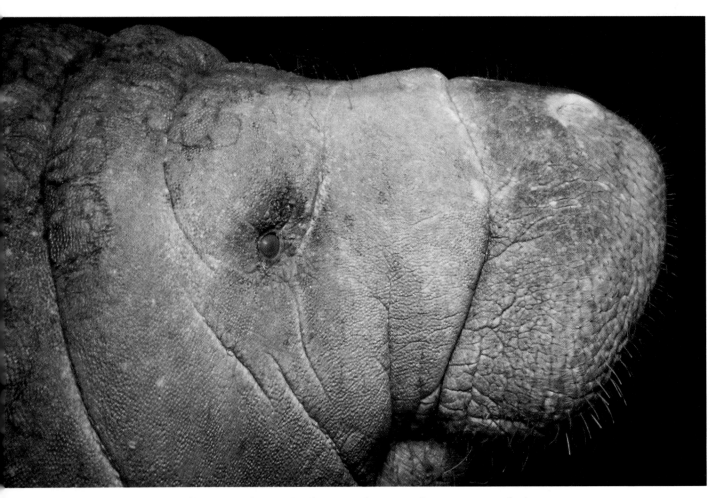

Manatees can see well, even through the membranes that protect their eyes.

Manatees have excellent hearing, which helps them when cloudy water impairs their vision.

Although a manatee's eyes are able to see clearly, murky water can make seeing difficult. Fortunately, manatees hear very well. In addition to the sounds people can hear, manatees can hear **infrasounds,** sounds with pitches too low for humans to hear. Manatees don't have outer ears. Instead, they have an ear opening on each side of the head, slightly behind the eyes. The ear openings are only about the size of a pencil point, but their small size doesn't lessen the manatee's hearing ability.

Manatees may also "hear" sounds in another, special way. They have large, oily cheekbones that touch their well-developed ear bones. Biologists think that sound waves may pass through a manatee's cheekbones directly into its ear bones, bypassing the outer ear opening.

Biologists are still studying manatees' senses of taste and smell. Manatees have taste buds on their tongues, and when offered choices in food, they show preferences for certain plants. Together, their senses of taste and smell seem to help them distinguish healthy plants from poisonous ones. It appears that manatees also use taste and scent to recognize other manatees and to identify females who are ready to mate.

A manatee feasts on water hydrilla.

SIMPLE NEEDS

Manatees are **herbivores,** animals that eat plants. Sea grasses, water hyacinths, some types of algae, and water hydrilla are among the manatee's first-choice foods. Florida manatees also eat mangrove leaves. West African manatees will eat fruits such as cassavas if they fall into the water.

Shrimps, fishes, and small crabs often live around the plants manatees eat. If these animals happen to be among the plants a manatee shoves into its mouth, they become part of the meal. Wild manatees have been seen eating fish, and if captive manatees are offered a fish, they may eat it. Still, their diet is usually confined to aquatic plants.

A manatee eats between 4 and 10 percent of its body's weight per day. For a 1,200-pound (540-kg) manatee, that's as much as 120 pounds (54 kg) of plants. So it's not surprising that up to 8 hours of a typical day are spent searching for food.

Aquatic plants grow throughout the waterways that West Indian manatees inhabit: on the bottom, on the surface, and in the middle. West Indian manatees feed on plants in all three locations. West African and Amazonian waters have fewer bottom-growing plants, so those species spend less time foraging along the bottom than West Indian manatees do. That's why the skull bones of West African and Amazonian manatees slant downward less than those of West Indian manatees.

Manatees sometimes seek food outside the water, too. If branches that hang over the water have tasty-looking leaves, manatees will munch on them. Manatees may also haul themselves partially out of the water to reach plants growing on the banks.

Once a manatee finds plants to eat, its upper lip plays an important role in getting the meal into its mouth. The upper lip is divided into two separate halves. Each half can grasp plants and pull them into the mouth. Sensitive **vibrissae** (vy-BRIH-see)—short, stiff, whisker-like hairs on the lips and snout—help manatees locate food. When plants brush against the vibrissae, the manatee can feel the movement and sense which direction it should move its lips.

Left: *Munching on sea grass*
Above: *Vibrissae*

25

Manatees don't have front teeth. Instead, horny, ridged pads at the front of the upper and lower jaws crush plants into pieces. The pieces are pushed toward the back of the mouth, where large, flat teeth called **molars** grind them up. Manatees have between 24 and 32 molars.

Eating grass puts a lot of wear on teeth. The leaves and stems of some species of grasses contain particles of **silica,** a very hard, glassy mineral. Sand is often made of silica. Chewing these plants wears away a tooth's surface like sandpaper wears away wood.

All this wear and tear would eventually leave a human toothless, but manatees can replace their worn-out teeth in an unusual way. New molars push up through the manatee's gums at the back of its mouth, then move toward the front. The movement is similar to that of a supermarket checkout's conveyor belt, only much slower. The molars move at a rate of 0.04 to 0.08 inches (1–2 mm) per month. Each molar is connected to the tooth in front of it by strong fibers. Biologists think these fibers help pull the new molars forward.

By the time a tooth reaches the front of the manatee's mouth, it has been worn down by months of chewing and its roots have been absorbed by the manatee's body. Without roots to hold it in place, the tooth loosens and falls out.

As this manatee chews on an anchor line, you can see that it has ridged pads instead of front teeth. Also notice how the manatee's upper lip is divided in two.

A log on the bottom of a waterway makes a good napping spot.

All manatees have a thick layer of fat to draw on for nourishment when food is scarce. Biologists have found that Amazonian manatees can also **fast,** or go without eating, for almost 7 months. The ability to fast is an **adaptation,** or a change made in response to living conditions. Some of the lakes Amazonian manatees inhabit undergo yearly wet and dry cycles. A lake's water level may drop by as much as 50 feet (15.2 m) during a dry period. Many aquatic plants die, leaving little for manatees to eat. During these dry periods, Amazonian manatees draw on their body fat for nourishment. If a dry season lasts longer than about 200 days, manatees may starve to death.

In addition to food, manatees need freshwater to drink. They can go without drinking for long periods, but they must eventually find freshwater to survive. Rivers, lakes, and springs that flow into oceans fill this need.

Like other animals, manatees need rest. When they aren't eating, they spend much of their time (2–12 hours per day) resting and sleeping. A resting manatee may "float" just beneath the water's surface or recline with its snout, flippers, and tail touching the bottom of the waterway. When the manatee rises to breathe, only its nostrils emerge from the water.

Manatees spend most of their time fulfilling their needs for food, water, and rest. The rest of a manatee's day is spent swimming and socializing with other manatees it meets. Manatees may swim 18 to 25 miles (29–40 km) per day or even farther. Although manatees may stay in the same area for weeks at a time, they also sometimes wander far beyond their normal range. In 1995, biologists tracked a Florida manatee they named Chessie. He traveled about 1,000 miles (1,600 km) from Florida all the way to Rhode Island—definitely a long summer trip!

Manatees have one more important need: they must live in warm water. If they remain in water that is too cold for too long, they will die. Amazonian manatees live in waters that don't cool down too much, but when the water temperature becomes lower than 69 to 72°F (21–22°C), West Indian manatees must search for warmer water. West African manatees can tolerate temperatures to about 64°F (18°C). If manatees live in areas where the water temperature drops as the winter months approach, they **migrate,** or travel, to warmer waters.

Rivers in warm, sunny climates make great homes for manatees.

Power plants produce warm-water havens for manatees.

SOCIAL LIFE AND RAISING YOUNG

Except for the time when they are ready to mate and produce young, manatees don't live in herds, or large groups that stay together for long periods of time. The quest for warm waters, however, can bring manatees together. They often gather by the dozens near hydroelectric plants. The heated water that these plants discharge is especially appealing to cold manatees.

Manatees are friendly with the other manatees they meet.

Manatees get along well in groups and are fun to watch. They clasp flippers and roll together, almost as if they were dancing. Because the sense of touch is important to manatees, they often nibble and groom each other.

Groups of manatees seem to enjoy playing games, including one that looks like follow-the-leader. The players move together in smooth patterns of diving, swimming, and breathing. Their motions are well coordinated, so each manatee must know what the others will do next. Biologists don't yet know how this information is communicated, but they think the manatees may use infrasounds.

Manatees vocalize with chirps, squeals, squeaks, and whistles. The loudness, length, and pitch of the noises vary. Manatees make sounds when they are playing or frightened, as well as to greet new arrivals in a group and to maintain contact between a mother and her baby. Biologists are still studying how manatees use sounds to communicate.

Manatees form groups at another time in their lives—when they are ready to mate and produce young. Females, or **cows,** are ready to bear young when they are 5 to 9 years old. Males, or **bulls,** are ready to mate when they are about 6 to 10 years old.

Although manatees can breed any time of year, they generally time their breeding so that the baby, or **calf,** will be born when food is plentiful. The mother needs a good food supply so her body can make milk for the calf. Most Florida manatees are born during the spring and summer.

When a cow is in **estrus,** or the period of time when she can become pregnant, about 6 to 20 bulls gather around her to form a **mating herd.** The bulls try to edge each other out of the way as they seek an opportunity to mate with the cow. The older and stronger bulls are more likely to succeed than their younger, smaller rivals. Mating can take place either at the surface or underwater. During a cow's estrus, which lasts from 2 to 4 weeks, she will mate with several bulls.

When the cow is no longer in estrus, the members of the mating herd go their separate ways. Bulls play no part in raising the calf. The cow will not mate again until her calf is grown, unless it dies while very young. The usual amount of time between calves is 2 to 3 years.

A mating herd of males competes for the attention of a lone female.

Gestation, or the amount of time it takes for the calf to develop inside the cow, lasts between 12 and 13 months. In the wild, a cow will find a quiet area where she can be alone to give birth. But in captivity, cows have been observed and photographed while giving birth. The captive calves were born both head first and tail first. Cows usually give birth to one calf; twins are rare.

A rare sight: a mother manatee with twin calves

This hungry calf looks as though it might be biting its mother, but it is actually nursing from the nipple under her flipper.

Newborn calves vary slightly in size. West Indian newborns weigh about 60 to 70 pounds (27–32 kg) and are 4.0 to 4.5 feet long (1.2–1.4 m). Amazonian newborns are smaller—about 2.5 feet long (0.8 m)—and weigh less.

A newborn calf's first task is to get oxygen. Within minutes of birth, the calf can swim and make its way to the surface. The cow often swims alongside it. From then on, the calf's place is next to its mother, where it swims behind her flipper. There, the calf **nurses,** or drinks milk, from the thumb-sized nipple located under the cow's flipper.

Manatees are watchful mothers, always staying near their calves.

Manatee milk contains a lot of fat and proteins, so calves gain weight rapidly—2 pounds (1 kg) or more per week. Calves are born with teeth and begin to munch on plants within 2 to 3 months of birth. (A calf's molars begin to move as soon as it starts to eat solid food.) Calves usually are weaned, or stop nursing, by the end of their first year or shortly after. If a cow dies before its calf is weaned, another nursing cow may adopt the orphaned calf and nurse it.

The bond between a cow and her calf is a strong one. A calf stays with its mother up to 2 years. During that time, they are together constantly. They call to one another frequently to make sure each knows where the other is. The calf relies on its mother to teach it how and where to find food. By migrating with her, the calf also learns the routes to warm waters.

Unlike many animal mothers, a manatee cow does not attack intruders that threaten her young. She will swim between her calf and the threatening animal if necessary, but manatees have no teeth or claws for fighting. So the cow and calf's first choice is always to swim away quickly. While in flight, they keep up a steady stream of calls to each other.

At about 2 years of age, a calf is ready to head off on its own. Often, it still maintains some contact with its mother, and it may live in nearby water. If the calf is lucky, it will have a long and healthy life—manatees may live more than 50 years.

Unfortunately, many manatees will not be lucky. Sharks and crocodiles sometimes kill West African manatees, and Amazonian manatees have been killed by jaguars. But only human beings regularly hurt or kill large numbers of manatees. And if we do not act more responsibly than we have in the past, there is a very real danger that all manatee species will become extinct.

Crocodiles (left) *sometimes kill West African manatees, and Amazonian manatees have to watch out for jaguars* (right).

In some cases, sirenians can be hunted legally. At left, Australian aboriginals capture a dugong under traditional hunting rights.

PEOPLE AND MANATEES

For hundreds of years, people have hunted manatees. A manatee's meat could feed many people. Its tough hide made strong shields and leather cords. Its oily fat was used as fuel for lamps. Bones were made into medicines and carved into jewelry. Manatees were hunted intensely through the first half of the 1900s, particularly in South America and North America. The number of manatees got lower and lower.

To protect the remaining manatees, many countries have set up national parks and **sanctuaries,** guarded areas where hunting is not allowed. Unfortunately, poaching, or illegal hunting, still occurs in many places in South America and West Africa—even in national parks and sanctuaries. Although about 45 nations have laws protecting manatees, the laws are often not well enforced. Many countries simply don't have enough money to hire rangers to patrol the sanctuaries.

In some places, starvation is a devastating reality, especially during long, dry periods when crops won't grow. Faced with starvation, the people who live in these areas may be forced to kill manatees illegally. Another problem is that in parts of Africa, hunting manatees is a traditional and valued custom. It is not easy, and it takes time, to change people's minds about long-standing customs.

Illegal hunting is not the only cause of manatee deaths. Manatees die accidentally when they become entangled in fishing nets and drown. They may also die from swallowing fishhooks and trash that have been tossed into the water. Many dams have floodgates, doors that control the flow of water. Closing floodgates have killed manatees. In canals, manatees can be hurt or killed by the navigation locks used to raise and lower water levels for boat traffic.

Some boaters kill manatees by driving too fast or failing to watch for them. In Florida, about one-fourth of all manatee deaths are caused by motorboat propellers. The skin of many Florida manatees is crisscrossed with propeller scars. In fact, the Sirenia Project of the U.S. Geological Survey maintains a catalog that shows the scar patterns of more than 1,200 manatees. This catalog is one of the tools biologists use to identify individual manatees for study.

People often use chemicals to kill weeds and insects on lawns, on fields, and in waterways. When these chemicals are washed into the water and absorbed into manatees' bodies, some can harm the animals. The same thing can happen when sewage, or waste material, is released into waterways.

Above and right: *Manatees are often injured by boat propellers.*

Development along the Crystal River in Florida has taken living space away from manatees.

We also hurt manatees in another, less recognizable way. Each year, people destroy more and more of the manatee's habitat. For example, in Florida and other southern coastal states, people are building homes and other structures close to the water. In some places, water is drained away to create new land for home sites. That means manatees can't live there anymore. In Brazil, mangrove swamps have been drained for farms, leaving less food and habitat for Amazonian manatees.

Cutting down trees also creates a problem. Soil is no longer held in place by tree roots, so storms can carry it into the water. The extra soil makes the water cloudy and blocks sunlight from reaching aquatic plants. In Florida's Tampa Bay, 80 percent of the sea-grass beds have disappeared during the last few decades. That means a lot less food for manatees.

Although people are the biggest threat to manatees' survival, they do die from other causes. During the first four months of 1996, more than 150 Florida manatees were killed by a **red tide.** Red tides are caused by a tiny, reddish organism that grows in water. When very large numbers of this organism grow, they turn the water red. Red tide organisms are swallowed by fishes and other tiny aquatic animals, such as those that live around the plants manatees eat. When manatees eat those animals, they become sick. Biologists think the Florida manatees died as a result of swallowing red-tide-infected animals along with mouthfuls of plants.

In areas where lots of manatees live, signs warn boaters to watch carefully for them.

No matter what the cause, each manatee death increases the danger of extinction. But people are doing several things to reduce the number of deaths and make the species' future brighter. For example, the government of Florida has declared the entire state a manatee sanctuary. The Florida Manatee Sanctuary Act of 1978 made it illegal to "annoy, molest, harass, or disturb any manatees."

Florida has also developed the Manatee Recovery Plan, a list of tasks that people and governments can carry out to help manatees survive. The tasks include establishing and enforcing boat speed zones, educating people about manatees, working to preserve manatee habitat, and creating safe warm-water areas for manatees, especially along Florida's southeastern coast, where manatee populations are declining.

Florida manatees can seek shelter in several places. Blue Spring State Park, Homosassa Springs State Wildlife Park, and the Crystal River National Wildlife Refuge are safe, patrolled places where manatees live. Some parks do not allow motorboats. Those that do have strict speed limits. In the winter, when manatees gather in warm areas, people are not allowed to harass them. As a result, the manatee populations in Blue Spring and Crystal River are increasing.

Above: *This manatee is just outside the boundary of the Crystal River sanctuary.*
Right: *Buoys mark the sanctuary for boaters and swimmers.*

Above: *Propeller guards can reduce injuries to manatees in low-speed collisions with boats.*
Right: *An injured calf is fitted with a special wetsuit by a care worker at SeaWorld of Florida.*

Scientists are working on ways to solve other problems that threaten manatees, such as closing floodgates. Engineers are testing gate protectors that use sound waves or electric sensors to detect the presence of manatees. When a manatee disturbs the sensor, the floodgate stops closing and pauses before starting again.

Zoos and oceanariums, or large aquariums, are sponsoring programs to help manatees all over the world. Oceanariums provide safe homes to orphaned calves, which have no mothers to teach them migration routes and the location of grazing areas. Oceanariums also provide temporary shelter for injured or sick manatees. While the manatees heal, biologists study their body chemistry and behavior. When possible, the manatees are released into their home area after they recover. Those that can't be released usually adapt well to captivity.

Many people will never have the opportunity to see a live manatee. That doesn't mean they shouldn't be concerned about what happens to manatees. We are just beginning to learn how important it is to maintain healthy **ecosystems,** or communities of plants and animals. For an ecosystem to survive, all of its members must remain healthy. For example, manatees produce **feces,** or waste materials, that nourish many plants and animals. If manatees become extinct, these plants and animals will be affected. Many ecosystems overlap each other, so the manatee's ecosystem may even affect ours in ways we aren't aware of.

Most people will only have the chance see a live manatee at an aquarium or observatory, such as this one at the Homosassa Springs State Wildlife Park.

The survival of manatees, such as these two in the Crystal River in Florida, lies in our hands.

Saving manatees from extinction is up to us. It won't be an easy job, and it will require research, planning, and hard work. We must think about the way we live and how our actions affect other kinds of life. Preserving and protecting manatees is a goal worth pursuing. And each life saved brings us one step closer.

GLOSSARY

adaptation: a change made in response to living conditions

aquatic: living in water

bull: a male manatee

calf: a baby manatee

cervical vertebrae: spinal column bones found in the neck area

cones: tiny, light-sensitive cells that are found in the eye and help animals distinguish colors

cow: a female manatee

ecosystem: a community of plants and animals that interact with each other and their environment

endangered: at risk of disappearing forever

estrus: the time when a female manatee can become pregnant

extinct: when all members of a type of animal or plant have died out

fast: to go without food

feces: solid waste produced by an animal

gestation: the amount of time it takes for an unborn animal to develop inside its mother's body

habitat: the place where an animal normally lives and grows

herbivores: animals that eat plants

infrasounds: sounds with pitches too low for humans to hear

mammals: animals that feed their young with milk from their own bodies

mating herd: a group of manatees made up of several males and a female that is ready to become pregnant

migrate: to travel from one place to another as the seasons change

molars: large, flat teeth that manatees use to grind plant pieces

nictitating membrane: a tissue that slides up over the eye of a swimming manatee to provide protection

nurse: to drink milk from a mother's body

red tide: water that has been turned red by a large group of tiny, reddish life forms. Red tides can kill sea animals.

rods: tiny, light-sensitive cells that are found in the eye and help animals see well in dim light

sanctuary: a guarded area where animals are protected from hunting

silica: a very hard, glassy mineral found in some plants manatees eat

species: a type of plant or animal

vibrissae: short, stiff, whisker-like hairs, located on a manatee's lips and snout, that help the animal locate food

INDEX

ABOUT THE AUTHOR

Sally M. Walker is the author of numerous science books for children, including *Earthquakes, Rhinos, Hippos, Sea Horses,* and *Dolphins,* all published by Carolrhoda Books. Although her favorite job is writing, Ms. Walker also works as a children's literature consultant and has taught children's literature at Northern Illinois University. While she writes, Ms. Walker is usually surrounded by her family's golden retriever and two cats, who don't say very much but provide good company. She lives in Illinois with her husband and two children.

Photographs are reproduced through the courtesy of: **Tom Stack and Associates:** (© Brian Parker) front cover, back cover, pp. 4–5, 10 (top left), 13, 19, 20, 21, 36 (both), 44–45, (© Thomas Kitchin) p. 9 (top right), (© Gary Milburn) p. 9 (bottom right), (© John Shaw) p. 9 (top left), (© Jeff Foott) p. 16, (© David Young) p. 39, (© Matt Bradley) p. 41 (bottom right); **Innerspace Visions:** (© Doug Perrine) pp. 2, 6–7, 10 (bottom left), 15 (top right), 17 (left), 18, 22, 23, 24, 25 (both), 26, 27, 28, 30, 31, 32, 33, 34–35, 38 (both), 41 (top), 42 (both), 43, (© David B. Fleetham) p. 8, (© Fernando Trujillo) p. 15 (bottom left), (© Ben Cropp Productions) p. 37; © Frank Staub, p. 9 (bottom left); © Lou Bopp, p. 10 (bottom right); © Pieter Folkens/Marine Mammal Images, p. 12; © William Muñoz, p. 17 (top right); © Patrick M. Rose/Save the Manatee Club, p. 29; © Jeff Foott, p. 40. Illustrations on pp. 11 and 14 by Laura Westlund, © 1999 Carolrhoda Books, Inc.

Gr. 3-6